CHANO

I am Chano the Chili Man.

I sell my chilies as fast as I can.

Loaded with chilies to the sky,

people wave at my truck as I go by.

My best chilies come from New Mexico.

I sell them to people wherever I go.

Roast them, toast them, put them in a pan.

Peel them and eat them, if you can.

Hot chilies, mild ones – it doesn't matter.

Put them on tacos or onto a platter.

From parent to child for generations,

chilies have a place in our celebrations.

Thread them on strings, hang them to dry.

They make decorations that please the eye.

Red chilies, green chilies, yellow ones, too –
I have chilies just right for you.

I'm Chano the Chili Man.